PHOTOGRAPHIC MEMORIES

of

DEVON & CORNWALL

Front cover picture:
Clovelly, Main Street in 1894 (33490)

Above:
Looe Harbour in 1912 (64624)

FRANCIS FRITH AND HIS
UNIQUE ARCHIVE

In 1860, Francis Frith, the Quaker son of a Chesterfield cooper, was 38 years old. He had already sold a massive grocery business he had built up, for a small fortune. Like Livingstone and Stanley, Frith was fired with a romantic Wanderlust, and the Victorian deep passion for travelling and exploring. Between 1857 and '59 he made several pioneering photographic journeys to remote regions of the Nile that brought him considerable fame.

After his marriage in 1860, he confined his wanderings a little closer to home and began a series of photo trips around Britain. His aim was to make his pictures available to the greatest number of people possible - life was hard and drab for millions of Victorians, and Frith believed his 'view souvenirs' of seaside resorts, beauty spots and town and village scenes would help keep their rare days out alive in their memories. He was right: by 1890 he had created the largest photographic publishing company in the world!

As well as thousands of views of high streets around Britain, Frith's growing archive included beautiful scenes of leafy glades, dusty lanes, rocks and coastlines, and the boats and riversides, beloved of Victorian wanderers like Jerome K Jerome - whose 'Three Men in a Boat' had struck a strong chord with the public.

Life in the Frith family was never dull. The family went with him on many trips, and the highlights were recorded by his wife, Mary Ann, in her journal. In 1872 she tells of a relaxing three week expedition to Ilfracombe in North Devon. Whilst such trips may have been something of a holiday for his wife and children, Francis Frith found no time to put his feet up. He was up and down the coast photographing Barnstaple and Lynton, hiring carters to carry him out to remote locations, and boatsmen to row him round the bay to view and photograph spectacular cliff formations.

After Francis Frith died in 1898 his sons carried on the business for many years with great success, specialising in postcards and other prints. So impressive is the archive he started that **The Financial Times** called it *'a unique and priceless record of English life in the last century'*.

PHOTOGRAPHIC MEMORIES

OF

DEVON & CORNWALL

THE FRANCIS FRITH COLLECTION

This edition published by
The Francis Frith Collection exclusively for
Selectabook Ltd., Roundway, Devizes,
Wiltshire SN10 2HR

First Published in 1996

© The Francis Frith Collection

ISBN 1 85937 021 7

Printed in Italy by Imago Publishing

Reproductions of all the photographs in this book
are available as framed or mounted prints from
The Francis Frith Collection at the address below.
Please quote the town, full title and negative number
shown in brackets.

The Francis Frith Collection
The Old Rectory, Bimport, Shaftesbury, Dorset SP7 8AT
Tel: 01747 855669 Fax: 01747 855065

CONTENTS

H ONITON is famous for its pottery and lace-making, which was brought here by Huguenot Flemish refugees. The town's fine old main street is one of the straightest and widest streets in England; a veritable market place in its own right. It never fails to make an impression on visitors entering Devon for the first time along the A30.

Top: Honiton laceworker in 1908 (58076) Honiton lace, which is similar to Brussels lace, was worn by Queen Charlotte at her wedding to King George III in 1761. **Above: High Street, Honiton in 1904** (52109) The main street of Honiton is lined with Georgian shops and houses, built after fires had destroyed most of the town in the 18th century. In the middle of the street there is a modern church in Norman style, built in the last century, with a tower rising over 100 feet and six bells.

Above: Station Road, Axminster in 1902
(48456) The little girl in a pinafore and hat is too preoccupied with her perambulator to notice the cameraman.

Left: Trinity Square, Axminster in 1902
(48453) Axminster is believed to be the site of the battle of Brunanburgh in 937 AD when King Athelstan won a decisive victory over the Danes. Athelstan was so concerned about the souls of seven Earls who were put to death in the battle that he gave the church of Axminster 'seven priests to serve God for their soules'. The carpet industry for which Axminster was renowned 'for there were none better in England' was moved to Salisbury in the 19th century. In the photograph, some older children pose for the cameraman in the town's main square.

Top: South Street, Axminster in 1902 (48454) The wide variety of architectural styles in this street are evidence of the long history of this small town and provide a picturesque setting for this coy little girl with her shopping basket who obviously had nothing to fear from the traffic. **Above: Axminster in 1902** (48449) On rising ground beside the River Axe this ancient and peaceful small market town huddles round the church. Near the church is Court House, where Axminster's world famous carpets were made.

BEER. Although Beer is a simple fishing village nestling in the bottom of a combe its past has not been without moments of excitement. Its inhabitants, who were renowned for supplementing their income by smuggling, are believed to have Iberian blood in their veins after the crew of a wrecked Spanish ship settled in the village and married village girls. The stone for Exeter Cathedral came from nearby quarries.

Right: Beer beach in 1898 (42434) The many small, single masted clinker built fishing boats pulled up on the shingle beach are evidence that Beer was a very busy fishing village.

Above: Beer in 1892 (31318) In the doorways of their thatched cottages and quaint old houses the women of Beer made the lace for Queen Victoria's wedding dress, costing £1000. Somewhere in the village is the home of Jack Rattenby, a smuggler turned privateer, who had a scarlet pimpernel's ability to avoid arrest.

SIDMOUTH. Lying in a sheltered spot, where the River Sid trickles to the sea between cliffs of warm, pink rock, Sidmouth was a fashionable resort in the early 19th century. With a climate mild enough for eucalyptus trees the town was thought to be a good wintering spot for those with weak chests and throats. It was also famous for its Mrs Partington, who was held up by politicians as an example of determination when, following the great storm of 1828, she tried unsuccessfully to sweep the sea from her house with a mop.

Right: Sidmouth High Street in 1906 (53807) The town gathers compactly around the church and was greatly favoured by Queen Victoria's father, the Duke of Kent who, being relatively impoverished, stayed in Woolbrook Cottage, later renamed Royal Glen.

Above: Sidmouth, Fore Street in 1904 (52071) Carriages and handcarts were the only traffic hazards in this busy street and hats defined one's status in life. No one went without a hat and wearing the right one was important. Indeed, to describe someone as a 'bad hat' was seriously derogatory. While the 'knobs' passed in their stagecoach, a man collected 'any old iron' with a handcart.

Top: Sidmouth Esplanade in 1918 (68739) To the East, past the elegant pillared terrace of the Royal York Hotel, one sees Beer head, where the rugged coastline of Devon gives way to the white chalk cliffs of Southern England. **Above: Sidmouth looking West in 1924** (76360) Queen Victoria first saw the sea at Sidmouth. Her father, the Duke of Kent, would frequently carry her onto the beach in his arms and show her to visitors whom he begged to "look on her well for she is to be your Queen."

OTTERY ST MARY's most famous son was the poet Samuel Taylor Coleridge who was born either in the vicar's house or in the schoolmaster's house. His father was both. The church in which his father preached was not only noted for its great size, but also for having an unusual mediaeval clock, made three centuries before Gallileo, in which the sun, moon and stars revolved around the earth.

Right: Market Place, Ottery St Mary in 1907 (58182) On a warm sleepy summer day, W Hake and Co, general milliners and drapers, protect their stock in the sunny Market Place with canvas blinds. Horse-drawn carts wait outside to make deliveries to customers.

Above: Talaton village in 1906 (56675) About four miles from Ottery St Mary is the village of Talaton where the village shop, on the right, would have been the week-day focus of village life. When very few people had cars or telephones and getting to town could be difficult, village shops met most people's daily needs and were the hub of village communications.

Above: Budleigh Salterton High Street, 1918 (68726) An attractive mix of shops and a higgledy piggledy style gave a warm and busy feel to the town's main shopping street which sloped down to the shingle beach made up of smooth, pink pebbles.

Left: Budleigh Salterton Promenade in 1898 (42448) This once fashionable resort had a distinct and somewhat retiring charm. On its seafront the Victorian painter Sir John Millais painted 'The Boyhood of Raleigh' depicting a sailor yarning to two small boys, one of whom, Sir Walter Raleigh, was born in the town in 1552. The sea wall which Millais used as the setting for the painting still stands.

EXETER. An ancient city with a proud history and a wonderful variety of buildings, Exeter was the only town in England to hold out for two years against William the Conqueror. Unfortunately, many of its fine buildings were destroyed by enemy bombing in the Second World War.

Right: The Guildhall, Exeter in 1930
(82292) Exeter's 15th century Guildhall is the oldest municipal building in England.

Below: The High Street, Exeter in 1896
(38012) This busy shopping street lies at the heart of a city which first became prosperous by seaborne trade. However, in the 13th century a weir was built across the river by the Countess of Devon which stopped ships reaching the town.

Opposite: Stepcote Hill, Exeter in 1911
(63678) This steep cobbled hill with its stepped pavement was part of the main thoroughfare through Exeter until Bridge Street was opened in 1778.

Above: St Mary's Steps Church, Exeter in 1912 (64577) Three figures, known locally as Matthew the miller and his two sons, strike the hours on the tower of St Mary's church on Stepcote Hill.

Left: Mol's Coffee House, Exeter in 1906 (53783) The first floor room of this famous coffee house, dating from Elizabethan times, was a favourite meeting place for sea captains.

Opposite above: Exeter in 1896 (38033) Seagoing ships of up to 300 tons were given access to Exeter in the 16th century by means of a five and a half mile canal.

Opposite below: The High Street, Exeter in 1900 (46043) A mix of relatively modern buildings and old houses graced by elegant lamp standards gave this street its famous vitality.

Previous page: The port of Exeter in 1896 (38034): A legal dispute over a weir built across the River Exe by the Countess of Devon in the 12th century lasted nearly 300 years. In 1564 the city commissioned England's first ship canal and vessels were once again able to reach the town.

Above: Rolle Street, Exmouth in 1895
(36055) On the sandy mouth of the River Exe, Exmouth is Exeter's seaside resort. Lying in one of the few flat areas of Devon, it has long been popular with those who find hill climbing tiring. Most of the buildings in this main shopping street were built in the 19th century when Exmouth was developed alongside the original parish of Littleham.

Left: The view from the Beacon, Exmouth in 1925 (78594) A pleasure craft negotiates the dangerous shifting sands of the Exe estuary. Turner, who was famous for his paintings of the different effects of light, came to this vantage point to paint the spectacular view of the sun setting over the South Devon coast.

REDITON. Once famous for the manufacture of woollen cloth and in more recent times for boots, sweets and pottery, Crediton was a pleasant and prosperous place. It was the home of St Boniface, an early Christian preacher who made it the seat of the first Bishop of Devon and Cornwall. The great size of its church led to the proud couplet "*when Exeter was a buzzy down, Kirton was a cathedral town*".

Top: The High Street, Crediton in 1904 (52085) Long and broad and on a slope, Crediton's main street had shops of every kind below pleasing Georgian facades. Before the days of radio and television, Barnes the newsagents would have been the main source of news on the latest events. **Above: The High Street, Crediton in 1896** (37634) In the 18th century Crediton suffered two serious fires in less than a generation. The major re-building that followed probably accounts for the street's consistency of style.

DAWLISH. About half-way along the five miles of attractive coastline between the Exe and the Teign estuaries lies Dawlish, a seaside resort with a good bathing beach and a mainline railway along the sea front. In tunnels constructed by Brunel, steam trains took visitors through the picturesque red cliffs and past strangely shaped rocks with names like The Parson and The Clerk, and brought prosperity to the town.

Right: Boat Cove, Dawlish in 1925 (78437) Pulled up on the beach are rowing boats and clinker built sailing dinghies reminiscent of Arthur Ransome's *Swallows and Amazons*. Behind the seafront, detached houses nestle in tree lined avenues.

Above: The beach, Dawlish in 1922 (72990) A long train stands on the sea front as people recline in deckchairs below the changing huts, but many were quite happy to remain in their skirts and long trousers. Only a few brave souls, and most of those children, donned swimming costumes to paddle and play in the water.

Above: Dawlish in 1928 (81171) Most of Dawlish's Victorian and Regency houses are not on the sea front but face inwards towards the burbling River Daw as it makes its attractive way over waterfalls and between well kept lawns through the heart of the town towards the sea.

Left: Whale Bones at Teignmouth in 1922 (73089) These massive whale bones were given to the town by Pike Ward "a man not given to sentiment" who had them erected on what was then called The Old Maid's walk. They provided the photographer with an irresistible frame for two fashion conscious ladies dressed in the long flapper designs popular in the 1920s.

Top: Teignmouth Parade in 1903 (49559) Enjoying a river aspect as well as a sea front, Teignmouth started to develop as a holiday resort in the 18th century. Among its early visitors was Jane Austen. Keats, who loved it, described it as a place "where close by the stream you may have your cream all spread on barley bread". **Above: Regent Street, Teignmouth in 1906** (54060) Outside the Triangle Restaurant on the right stands a 'horseless carriage' fitted with beautiful brass carriage lamps.

NEWTON ABBOT. The 'new town' of William de Brewer, a 13th century Abbot of Tor Abbey, Newton Abbot is a busy market town at the head of the navigable waters of the River Teign. It lost much of its heritage with the age of steam when the railway workshops were built here.

Right: Newton Abbot in 1906 (56573) The old, solitary, battlemented tower standing at the crossroads or Five Dials is all that remains of the mediaeval church of St Leonard which was dismantled in the 19th century.

Below: The Market in Newton Abbot in 1926 (78550) The highlight of the week was the Wednesday market when local farmers exercised their eye for a good animal. In the background, buyers and sellers huddle round cattle pens trying to catch the auctioneer's attention with signals so slight that others will not notice. On the left is the pannier market where fruit and vegetables are sold on Wednesdays and Saturdays.

ORBAY is bordered by three towns, each with its own specific character. No doubt Torquay is the grandest, but Paignton is a truly family resort, while Brixham, which grew from a working fishing village, is picturesque. Torquay's development started in the early 19th century when, during the Napoleonic Wars, the Navy used the bay as an anchorage and Naval officers began to move into the district. An equable climate brought to the town many wealthy people who were prevented from going abroad by the war and this led to the development of its elegant streets and attractive seaview terraces laid out by architects employed by the Palk family.

Right: Princess Parade, Torquay in 1920 (69579) A summer holiday in Torquay was a wonderful opportunity to wear the latest fashion. In blazer, white flannels and white shoes, this bare headed man clearly thought he was cutting quite a dash as he strolled the promenade with his lady friends.

Above: Torquay in 1924 (76401) Even on the beach, most people remained modestly covered and many wore hats. The bathing suit worn by the lady approaching the changing huts would have been considered quite daring by older people.

Top: The Harbour, Torquay in 1890 (25921) Increased Naval activity called for an extension of the harbour to provide a safe landing point for tenders as well as boats used for fishing and pleasure. **Above: Anstey's Cove, Torquay in 1896** (38609) In contrast to the bands and trams of Torquay, Anstey's Cove provided good bathing in clear water, protected by a reef. The hut on wheels is a bathing machine which was rolled into the sea. Bathers left their clothes in the hut and went straight down steps into the water.

Above: Fleet Street, near Torquay in 1906 (54027) Behind this genteel shopping street, with its practical system of supporting blinds to protect the stock from the sun, rise expensive hillside developments with superb sea views.

Left: Abbey Crescent, Torquay in 1896 (38598) In the Northern reaches of Torbay, well sheltered from the North and East winds, Torquay's gentle climate led to its development in the 19th century as the English Riviera. Terraces such as these gave the town a distinctly Mediterranean feel.

Opposite top: Cockington, near Torquay in 1901 (47821) Not far outside Torquay lies the hamlet of Cockington set in a deep wooded valley with an Elizabethan manor, ancient thatched cottages and its famous 14th century forge in the middle of the village. For many years visitors have bought lucky miniature horseshoes, beaten out by the blacksmith on the old anvil.

Opposite below: Cockington, Torquay in 1906 (54016)

Top: The Downs at Babbacombe in 1918 (68547) The view from the top of the cliff at Babbacombe embraces Maidencombe, Teignmouth, the mouth of the River Exe and on to Budleigh Salterton and Sidmouth. It provided a spectacular backdrop for this well attended evening concert. **Above: Babbacombe in 1926** (78446) Now on the fringes of Torquay, which has grown enormously since this photograph was taken, the poet Keats thought Babbacombe was the finest place he had seen in the South.

Above: Bathing beach at Paignton in 1896
(38545) Only three miles from Torquay, Paignton is a family resort with a sea front lined with hotels and guest houses and enjoying wonderful views of Torbay over the red sand beach. Changing huts on wheels, called bathing machines, which could be rolled into the water preserved the modesty of prim Victorians who, since Regency times, had been convinced of the health-giving benefits of sea bathing.

Left: Preston Sands, Paignton in 1918
(68533) In the early days of flying these light sea planes pulled up on the beach must have been quite a spectacle.

Overleaf: Church Street, Paignton in 1912
(64719) Behind the glamour of the town's sea front, the inhabitants of Paignton got on with the business of living and servicing the hotels and guest houses which were the town's main source of income. The parish church dedicated to St John looms over Church Street as a pony and trap, a common form of transport for those living out of town, passes Pook Bros, family butchers.

Top: The Promenade and Sands at Paignton in 1907 (58415A) A charabanc competes for passengers with a horse and carriage on Paignton's fashionable and busy sea front as people crowd around the bandstand for an afternoon concert. **Above: Brixham Harbour in 1926** (78490) In Brixham's inner harbour, which is more than 300 years old, sturdy fishing boats lie to their moorings. William of Orange landed here on his way to claim the throne and his statue faces landwards on the water's edge.

Above: Fore Street, Brixham in 1922
(73032) Visitors to Brixham did not
expect the sophistication of Torquay.
However, it did inspire its vicar Henry
Francis Lyte to write what is probably
the most famous hymn in the English
language, 'Abide With Me'.

Left: Bolton Cross, Brixham in 1922
(73033) Just opposite The Bolton Hotel,
cars stop outside the Public Hall and
New Market which was opened in 1866
to provide offices for the Council, the
School Board and the Harbour
Commissioners, as well as a new
Magistrate's Court and a hall capable
of accommodating 800 people.

Overleaf: Brixham in 1896 (38882)
A sturdy gaff-rigged fishing ketch makes
its way out of Brixham's old harbour.
The harbour was extended in 1916 by
the building of an 800 yard sea wall.
Behind the harbour, terraces of
fishermen's cottages climb up the hill.

TOTNES. According to local legend Brutus, the grandson of Aeneas of Troy, sailed up the River Dart to found both Totnes and the British race. In more recent times the town was noted for its fine hose and Daniel Defoe described it as "having more gentlemen than tradesmen of note". But even for the common man it was a good place to live, with enough salmon in the river to make the king of fish everyday fare.

Right: The High Street, Totnes in 1896 (38228) Slate fronted houses are common in the winding, narrow streets of this ancient town and provide a very effective and attractive weather-proofing finish for some of the older houses.

Below: Butterwalk, Totnes in 1896 (38227) The quaint colonnades in front of the shops in the Butterwalk are made variously of wood, iron and granite and remind one of Chester. This was where the fine hose of Totnes was sold at a time when the town was one of the chief clothing markets of England.

Above: Dartmouth in 1889 (21579) Since Richard the Lionheart left for his Crusade in 1189, ships and men have sailed out of this busy river to take part in nearly every British war. Near its mouth, Naval vessels mingle with pleasure yachts and fishing boats while the ferries go to and fro between Dartmouth and Kingsweir. At the top of the steep, wooded West flank of the river is the Britannia Royal Naval College.

Left: 'Totnes Castle', Totnes in 1896 (38216) From Totnes one could take pleasure cruises in smart, high-funnelled steamers to Dartmouth along the spectacular wooded valley of the River Dart.

Above: Fore Street, Kingsbridge in 1896 (38510) This view of the Kings Arms Hotel in Fore Street has changed little in over a hundred years. Built as a coaching inn in 1775, it retains much of its charm.

Left: Fore Street, Kingsbridge in 1896 (38429) Centre of a prosperous farming district known as the South Hams, Kingsbridge is a busy market town at the head of the tidal estuary which extends up from Salcombe. The old clock over the town hall with its four faces is similar to that of Cuckfield in Sussex.

Opposite above: Kingsbridge in 1920 (69826) Kingsbridge inlet penetrates deeply into the land and the octagonal stone spire of St Edmund's church was a landmark for ships coming up the estuary with rich cargoes.

Opposite below: The Bridge, Kingsbridge in 1890 (24525)

Top: Old Town Street, Plymouth in 1889 (22398) A hearse on rubber tyred wheels takes the corner between Old Town Street and Bedford Street going towards the Guildhall as a load of hay to feed horses stabled in the town comes from the direction of Tavistock.
Below: The Barbican, Plymouth in 1890 (22474) At the fishing quay along the side of Sutton Pool, the original port of Plymouth, heavy fishing smacks manoeuvre under sail. Their long bow sprits enabled them to carry a lot of canvas and they could move quickly when the wind was in the right quarter. Here landed Margaret of Anjou and Catherine of Aragon, future Queens of England.

Above: Royal Hotel, Devonport in 1890 (22446) It was George IV who, in 1824, changed the name of this great Naval dockyard town on the east bank of the River Tamar from Plymouth Dock to Devonport.

Left: Torpoint Ferry Bridge, Devonport in 1890 (22462) Foot passengers and horse drawn vehicles could cross to Cornwall by means of this chain ferry. Four miles upstream, Brunel's magnificent Royal Albert railway bridge spanned the River Tamar at 100 feet above the fast flowing waters to allow vessels with high masts to pass under it.

TAVISTOCK. Sir Francis Drake is Tavistock's most famous son. But the house on Crowndale Farm in which Britain's best known sailor since time began was born, has long gone and now, there is only a tablet to tell us where it stood. Tin mining and the woollen industry made Tavistock prosperous and its church, dedicated to St Eustace the Martyr, has an organ once played by Samuel Wesley and a window designed by William Morris.

Top: Duke Street, Tavistock in 1910 (62256) At quarter past eleven on a sunny summer's day a small child gets dangerously close to a pony while a perilously perched maid cleans the first floor windows of a shop. **Above: Duke Street, Tavistock in 1890** (22546) After the dissolution of the monasteries Henry VIII gave the land to his friends. Tavistock was given to John Russell, the first Earl of Bedford. The town's well kept streets and ample buildings testify to the care of successive Dukes of this line.

Above: Fore Street Market, Okehampton in 1890 (22590) The weekly market was not only an occasion for buying and selling, but a wonderful opportunity to catch up with the news. The fine granite tower at the end of the street is all that remains of a 15th century church rebuilt after a fire in 1842. At the very heart of Devon, Okehampton is the only place mentioned in the Domesday Book as possessing both a castle and a market.

Left: The Market, Okehampton in 1926 (82925) The life-size white hart on the porch of the Georgian White Hart Hotel faces Okehampton's handsome town hall and has welcomed travellers making their way North of the great moor for generations.

Above: Torrington, Market Place 1893 (32334) Also known as Great Torrington, Torrington existed chiefly on the manufacture of silk gloves and underwear, but it had a butter factory, and the weekly 'pannier market' (for butter, eggs, cream and poultry) was probably held in the market square, pictured above.

Left: Torrington Church in 1890 (24849) Torrington made history when, in the civil war, General Fairfax shut Royalist prisoners in the tower of the church which was being used as an arsenal. Fumbling about in the darkness, his prisoners accidentally set light to the gunpowder and the resulting explosion destroyed a large part of the church and killed 200 men. While the arcades and vestry of the present church are mediaeval, the tower and spire were built in the last century.

BARNSTAPLE has a Charter dating from the 10th century when it minted its own coins and claims to be the oldest borough in England. It was here that the diarist Samuel Pepys found the Huguenot girl who was to become his long-suffering wife.

Right: Boutport Street, Barnstaple in 1919 (69322) A lady negotiates with a street vendor in front of The Horse and Groom Inn.

Below: High Street, Barnstaple in 1894 (33422) The shops in this comfortable and reassuring High Street, with their elegant hanging signs and dignified fascias, reflect the quiet confidence of the late Victorian era.

Overleaf: Horse Fair, Barnstaple in 1923 (75164) In 1923 horses were still an important part of farm and village life and the annual horse fair held in September was a big occasion for those from the surrounding area. In towns, many people relied on horses and carts to make deliveries, particularly of bread and milk. But horse dealers enjoyed the same dubious reputation attached, in more recent times, to second-hand car dealers.

BIDEFORD. A prosperous port in the days of sail, Bideford was an export outlet for the cloth weavers of Devon as well as being an important ship building centre. The popularity of Charles Kingsley's book '*Westwood Ho!*', which he wrote in the Royal Hotel on the River Torridge's East bank, led to the development in the 1860s of a seaside resort here. Bideford's long, sandy beach was reputed to be one of the best in Devon.

Right: The Quay, Bideford in 1890 (24800) Sturdy, low waisted fishing smacks with heavy hemp rigging and canvas sails wait for the tide alongside Bideford's quay which is lined with elegant, three storey Georgian-style properties.

Above: High Street, Bideford in 1906 (55933) Narrow streets climb steeply from the quay in a town which straddles the River Torridge. **Opposite: The Quay, Appledore in 1923** (75146) In nearby Appledore, with its cobbled lanes, people devoted their time to boat building and fishing. This working quay would have been in use whenever the tide was high and was equipped with an unusual electric light standard.

ILFRACOMBE grew from a fishing village to become the largest holiday resort on the North Devon coast. Visited in the summer by paddle steamers from South Wales it was the only Devon town that many Welsh people knew. The port once enjoyed considerable importance, contributing six ships to the Navy of Edward III.

Right: Woolacombe in 1911 (63938) About four miles from Ilfracombe is the village of Woolacombe which looks out over the wide sweep of Morte Bay. On a clear day, it is possible to see Lundy Island 19 miles away.

Below: Ilfracombe in 1923 (74948) Thousands came to enjoy the resort's restfulness and beauty and to stay in the hotels and boarding houses ranked in terraces on the hill.

Opposite: Main Street, Clovelly in 1894 (33490) Sure footed donkeys fitted with panniers were used to negotiate this famous steep street, lined with flower-decked cottages. The street climbs 400 feet in only 200 yards.

TIVERTON's prosperity was founded first on wool and then on lace, giving the town an unusual number of good buildings. John Heathcote, who invented the bobbin machine to make lace, started the town's textile industry. R D Blackmore, the author of *Lorna Doone* was a pupil in the town's famous Blundell's School and gave Lorna's ardent admirer, John Ridd, his education there. The church has an organ case attributed to Grinlin Gibbons who carved the choir stalls for St Paul's cathedral.

Right: Castle Street, Tiverton in 1920 (69888) The stream running down the centre of the street was probably not very hygenic but held an inevitable fascination for small boys. The sandstone castle after which this street was named was once the home of the Courtenay family, Earls of Devon.

Below: St Paul's Street, Tiverton in 1920 (69889)

Opposite: Valley of Rocks Hotel, Lynton in 1907 (59372) This hotel takes is name from a smooth green hollow entered between Castle Rock and Ragged Jack in the peaks which rise behind Lynton. From the way in which the conductor is blowing his coach horn, the coach called 'Defiance', owned by T Copp, looks as though it is just about to depart with its valuable cargo of fashionable ladies.

LAUNCESTON once guarded the main route from Devon to Cornwall. It is a fine, unspoilt town with narrow streets and many Georgian houses surrounding a church and square. Set high above it is a castle from which one can look across Cornwall into Devon. But this lofty fortress, which was held by Parliament during the Civil War, is not just a decorative relic of the past, having been used as a military base in the last war.

Right: St Thomas's Church, Launceston in 1906 (56151) Standing by the River Kensey is this church with a fine old door hung on 600 year old hinges. It has a Norman font which is four yards round. The church was once the chapel of a priory which stood nearby from 1126 to 1539 and parts of the present building go back to the 13th century.

Above: Southgate Street, Launceston in 1906 (56130) Launceston originally had three gates, North, South and West, in the mediaeval wall which protected its inhabitants, but the only one still standing is the Southgate. To the East the town was protected by its imposing castle. During the plague the gates were firmly shut against strangers.

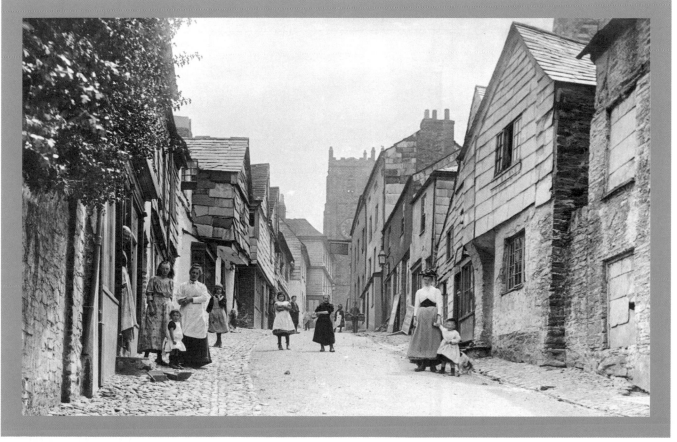

Top: St Stephens Church, Launceston in 1893 (32170) On the steep streets leading to the top of the town and St Mary's Church a crowd gathers to welcome the photographer. In the valley is St Thomas's Church and, breaking the skyline, the tower of St Stephen's.
Above: Launceston in 1893 (32166) At exactly mid-day, people wait outside their slate-hung houses in Northgate Street, leading up to the Jubilee Inn and St Mary's Church, for the baker as he makes his way towards them with baskets full of loaves.

ISKEARD is a little town with narrow streets on the edge of Bodmin moor. It was the childhood town of Robert Stephen Hawker, the famous vicar of Morwenstow, who was a writer and poet and one of the most talked-of parsons in the Church of England. One of the traits for which he was famous was his passionate devotion to the care of sailors shipwrecked on the Devon coast.

Right: St Keyne's Well, Liskeard in 1906 (56313) An idyllic country scene: a little girl watches men drawing water from the well underneath an old oak tree. The thatched cottage was probably the home of a farm worker.

Above: Barras Street Parade in Liskeard, 1893 (32347) Employees of the Devon and Cornwall Banking Company stand proudly outside their imposing premises in shirt sleeve order on a warm summer's day, while a horseman and carters pose in front of the fountain from which the public house in the background took its name.

Top: Webb's Hotel, Liskeard in 1890 (24463) Outside the hotel, removal contractor F J W Nicholls, who has come all the way from Plymouth, gives his horses their mid-day nosebags, while the little boy on the right has probably been deputed to fill a bucket with water from the fountain. An empty Hackney carriage awaits a client. **Above: Railway Station at Liskeard in 1907** (58796) Ladies dressed for travelling await the train near a kiosk displaying a poster for Pears' soap.

Bodmin was once the heart of Cornwall and its brownstone and granite faced buildings give it an air of authority. The town still has the county's biggest old church, built on the spot where St Guron lived as a hermit over 1400 years ago. Set at the entrance to one of Cornwall's most beautiful valleys, the town shares its name with the great moor which rises behind it.

Top: Fore Street, Bodmin in 1906 (56279) Behind the shops of Fore Street, Bodmin's 17th century Guildhall lies hidden. **Above: Fore Street, Bodmin in 1890** (24482) The building on the left with granite pillars surmounted by carved oxen heads was the town's central market. Built in the 19th century, it brought together for the first time all Bodmin's produce markets on a floor which is made of huge granite slabs. Today, the building houses a shopping arcade.

LOOE. Just below the junction of two wooded valleys the narrow Looe estuary separates the twin fishing towns of East and West Looe. With the river at their heart and the sea round the corner, one is never far from water in these well sheltered communities.

Right: West Looe Jetty in 1893 (32370) The crew of this two masted fishing vessel registered in Fowey are busy making sure that their nets are in good order.

Below: Looe in 1906 (56404) Fishermen of the future admire the view while the nets dry. In the background is the seven arched bridge, built in the 19th century, which brought both sides of the town together.

Overleaf: Looe Harbour in 1912 (64624) Adults and children watch from the quay wall as a small fishing boat negotiates the fast flowing tide.

POLPERRO is a tiny port lying between high rocky headlands. Its natural and unpretentious charm reflects the hard and dangerous business of fishing on which it depended for its livelihood.

Right: Polperro in 1907 (59269) On the first storey porch of the Pilchards Inn a man finds time to rest his feet with the newspaper, while below, another bewhiskered man, in fisherman's jersey and bowler hat, sits with a small boy who looks as though he could be his grandson.

Above: Polperro Harbour in 1888 (21268) After a journey through deep valleys and under an ancient bridge, the River Pol eventually arrives in this quaintest of harbours where small vessels can find protection from the Atlantic swell behind a short sea wall. **Opposite: Polperro in 1924** (76344) In rocky areas donkeys can prove more sure footed than horses and provide a valuable, if obstinate, means of transport.

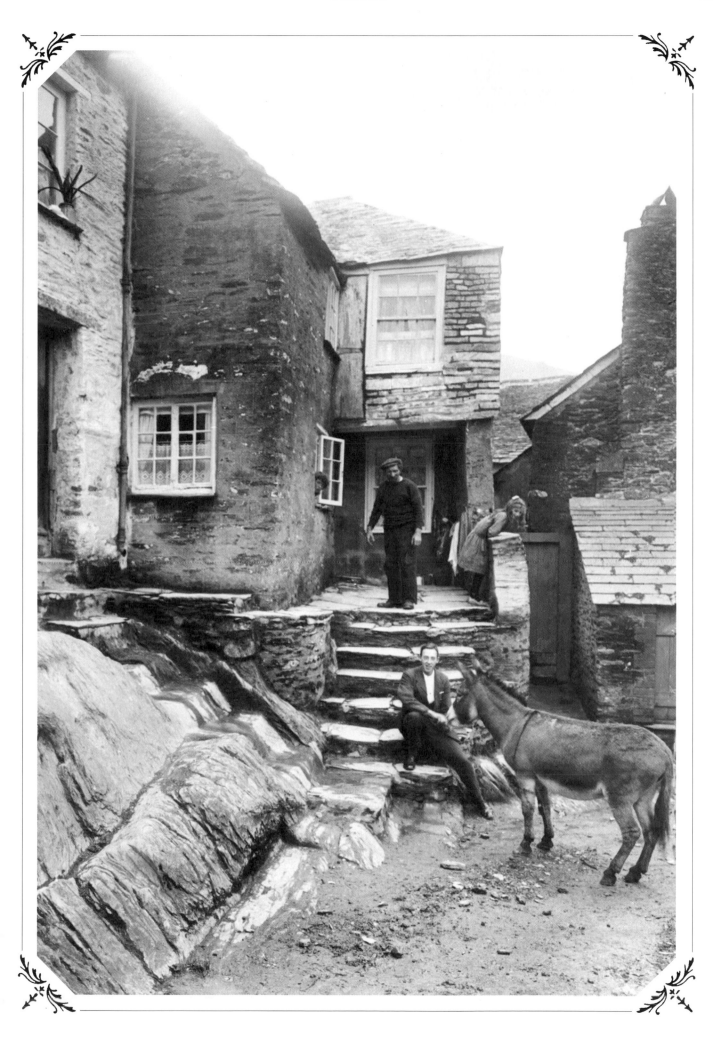

LOSTWITHIEL. In its mediaeval heyday, Lostwithiel housed the Stannary Parliament, Cornwall's proud claim to administrative independence from London. It was also the location of the Stannary Court for the Blackmoor tin mining district. Tin was brought to this Coinage town from the local mines to be taxed, assayed and marked.

Right: Bridge End, Lostwithiel in 1906 (56423) On the corner of one house in this old town there is a curious stone called 'the lease stone', on which a previous owner with aspirations of longevity had carved: *Walter Kendal of Lostwithiel was founder of this house 1658 Hath a lease of three thousand years which had beginning the 29th of September 1652.*

Above: North Street, Lostwithiel in 1906 (56422) The peaceful atmosphere of this quiet, traffic-free street, bordering the cemetery, is uplifted by the unusual domed cupola on the skyline. The oriel window of the house on the right has been prettily finished with stained glass, a form of decoration common in houses of this period.

Top: The Bridge at Lostwithiel in 1922
(73329) Five miles from the sea, the first
bridge across the River Fowey was built
in Lostwithiel in the 15th century. From
the mud on the banks, the photograph
was clearly taken somewhere near low
water. To reach the rowing skiff moored
in the centre of the river it is likely that
the owner had some sort of pulley
arrangement which allowed him to pull
the boat ashore. By picking his times to
go with the current he would probably
need to put little effort into an excursion
on the river.

Left: Parade, Lostwithiel in 1906 (56425)
Until the 16th century the River Fowey
was navigable to this point and the two
little boys dabbling their boots in the
water and the little boy in short trousers
standing by his shopping basket may be
on part of the old quay.

FOWEY. In Kenneth Grahame's famous book "*The Wind in the Willow*", Fowey is described by Sea Rat as 'the little, grey sea town that clings along one side of the harbour'. Kenneth Grahame was a frequent visitor to the town and was married in its parish church. He was no doubt familiar with its quays and jetties, which would have been busy with the export of china clay, and with its cobbled streets that come right to the water's edge.

Right: Town Quay, Fowey in 1888 (21250) From Town Quay a ferry crosses the picturesque creek to Boddinick on the west bank, saving a detour of more than ten miles to cross the first bridge across the river at Lostwithiel.

Above: Fowey in 1888 (21237) On the west side of the estuary is Boddinick. Its white-washed cottages and natural lanes have made it a favourite haunt of artists. **Opposite page: Fowey the Village in 1888** (21249) Around Fowey's mediaeval church, with its tower crowned with battlements and pinnacles, there is a maze of narrow streets. On the right is Varco, Fowey's watchmaker and jeweller.

ST AUSTELL. The green valleys of St Austell were turned into white hills following the discovery of china clay by the Quaker, William Cookworthy. As a result of this discovery, the town soon became the centre of one of Cornwall's most important industries.

Right: Truro Road, St Austell in 1920
(69783) At a time when the dangers of smoking were not as well known as they are today there were specialist tobacconists on many street corners.

Below: Fore Street, St Austell in 1920
(69785) At the heart of this busy town stands the parish church with a tower built of local yellow stone.

Opposite: The church of St Austell in 1890
(27626) The church is well known for the sculpted figures of the twelve apostles who stand in niches on three sides of its 90 feet tower.

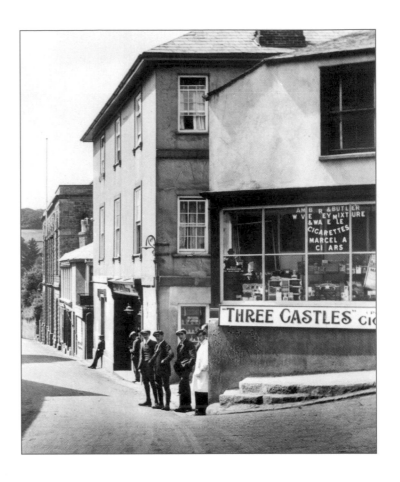

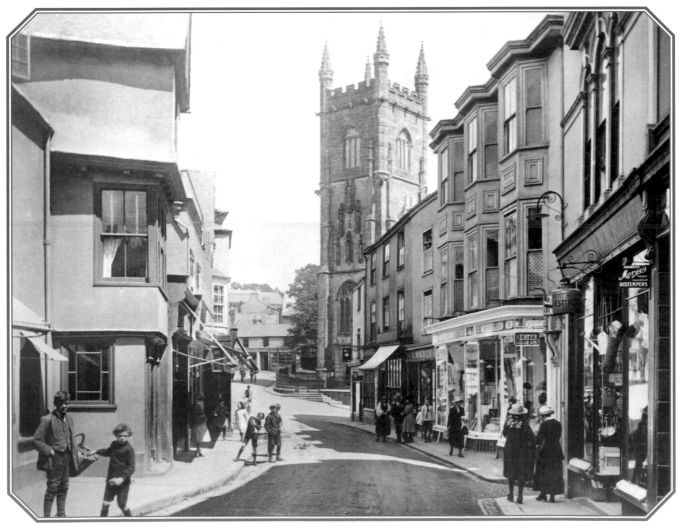

Top: Mevagissey Harbour in 1920 (69794) With steep, narrow streets and a sheltered harbour, Mevagissey has long been thought of as the most delightful of the small Cornish fishing towns. The fishing boat 'Diligent' looks as though it may have just returned from a fishing trip and a man leading a horse onto the quay is probably preparing to take the catch to market. **Above: The Inner Harbour, Mevagissey in 1890** (27557) While the tide is out and boats lie on the harbour floor, a group of youths use an upturned dinghy on the harbour wall for an informal meeting.

TRURO was granted a charter over 800 years ago and became Cornwall's cathedral city in 1877. Its imposing cathedral, completed in 1910, and its many fine Georgian buildings lend the city dignity as an administrative centre.

Right: Truro Cathedral from the river in 1903 (50854b) The spire of Truro cathedral soars over this small city and is reflected in the still waters of the river.

Below: Truro in 1897 (40594) Barclays Bank in Boscowan Street was originally built in 1888 as the West Cornwall Bank. It is faced with Carnsew granite worked in the Penryn Yard of Freemans.

Overleaf: Victoria Place, Truro in 1897 (40593)   There was great activity in Victoria Place on the day the photographer took this picture. In the entrance of Radmore's Dining Rooms a waitress in white pinafore and cap is curious to see what is going on. Further down the street, two small children play in the gutter outside Petworths, while outside Edwin Broad, the cash drapers with its decorative lamps, two ladies are probably discussing the advantages of different stuffs.

Top: Truro from the Viaduct in 1890 (23919) The central steeple of Truro Cathedral had yet to be built when this photograph was taken. **Above: Boscowen Street, Truro in 1912** (64732) The drinking fountain is near the spot where the bronze soldier, erected in memory of those who fell in the Great War, now stands. **Opposite: Truro Cathedral in 1912** (64729) Cornwall's memorial to Queen Victoria is the central steeple of Truro Cathedral. It is 250 feet high, one foot for every mile from London.

FALMOUTH. In 1688 Falmouth became the communications centre of the British Empire. Small, fast, heavily armed sloops carried Royal messages and bullion all over the world and information was sent to London by messengers on horseback because they could get there faster than a ship could sail up the English Channel. When the Packet Service was transferred to Southampton, Falmouth's fortunes declined but were revived when the railway began to bring in holiday-makers.

Right: Market Strand, Falmouth in 1890 (24208)

Opposite: Jacobs Ladder, Falmouth in 1908 (52227)
Rising out of The Moor, Jacobs Ladder with its 111 steps was installed in the 1830s by Jacob Hamblen, builder, tallow-chandler and property owner to connect businesses he had at the bottom of the hill with his property at the top.

Above: Falmouth in 1903 (50518) The Moor with the old Town Hall in the background. In front of the Packet Memorial and Methodist church, children play marbles. The Memorial was erected by public subscription in 1898 in memory of the gallant officers of HM Post Office Packet Service which operated from Falmouth from 1688 to 1850, but the plate on the memorial reads 1852.

Top: Falmouth from the docks in 1885 (8404) Falmouth is Britain's Southernmost port with a magnificent natural harbour and defences built by Henry VIII. In the age of sail, merchant ships called at Falmouth to receive their orders and to be told in which European ports they would find profitable markets for the cargoes they carried from all over the world. **Above: Falmouth Quay in 1908** (61059) Near the quay is the King's Pipe, a brick chimney where smuggled tobacco was burned when seized by excise men.

ELSTON is a typical Cornish town built of granite and slate. Almost the most Westerly town in Britain, the journey to London by horse and carriage could take nearly a week. Among the customs enjoyed by inhabitants and visitors alike is the May-time Furry or Floral Dance, a ceremony of pre-Christian origin when the streets are decorated with greenery.

Top: Coinage Hall Street, Helston in 1931 (84218) **Above: Coinage Hall Street, Helston in 1913** (65939) It is interesting to see the changes which took place in Coinage Hall Street over the eighteen years separating these two photographs which included the traumatic years of the Great War. While the external appearance of the Angel Hotel changed little, horses and carriages gave way to motor cars and fashions changed; men's jackets becoming looser-fitting and more casual, and not everyone wore a hat.

Top: Meneage Street, Helston in 1913 (65943) Shopkeepers and shoppers were happy to pose while the cameraman practised his craft. **Above: Coinage Hall Street, Helston in 1913** (65940) On the corner of Church Street and Coinage Hall Street stood the imposing Corn Exchange, now Helston's Guildhall. In the background Coinage Hall Street curves steeply down to the River Helford. On either side of the street there was a maze of alleys with quaint old shops and houses.

PENZANCE. With four miles of sandy beaches, sheltered by the cliffs of The Lizard and Land's End, and with possibly the mildest climate in Britain, it is hardly surprising that Penzance became a popular Regency watering place and winter resort. Famous for the view of St Michael's Mount, it is also the port for boats to The Scillies.

Right: The Promenade, Penzance in 1906
(56510) A walk on the Promenade was an opportunity for elegant ladies to play the fashionable game of seeing and being seen. At the time this phograph was taken, pinched waists were definitely in fashion.

Below: The Promenade, Penzance in 1906
(56510) Behind the sea front terraces, with their Victorian sash and bow windows and elegant gas lamp standards, rises the tower of Penzance's parish church.

Right: Quay Street, Penzance in 1906
(56515) A landmark for sailors, the
pinnacled tower of St Mary's church
looks out over grey slate roofs and the
masts of ships onto the lovely sweep of
Mount's Bay. In the streets below
children play games which have
remained unchanged over hundreds of
years while adults, one with a parasol,
pose self-consciously for the photograph
outside the Dock Hotel.

Above: Bedford-Bolitho Gardens, Penzance in 1920 (69737) Many exotic and subtropical plants and trees flourish in
Penzance's gentle climate and the town has some of the most beautiful gardens in England. This interesting garden with its
elaborate pergola and borders framed with local stone was a good place to sit on warm, sunny days. For times when the
weather was less clement, the wind shelter was often enough to enable hardy souls to continue to enjoy its beauty.

Above: Market Jew Street, Penzance in 1920 (69736) Hackney carriages wait outside Smiths, the 'hatter and clothiers' and people congregate outside Bailey's fish shop. Three small boys cast envious eyes at a man with a motor bike and sidecar whose head is only protected by a cap. This street leads to the Market House outside which there is a statue of Sir Humphrey Davy, inventor of the miner's safety lamp and one of Penzance's most famous sons.

Left: A Penzance fishwife in 1890 (27699) Most of the weight of the large basket of fish which this Penzance fishwife is carrying is borne on a band which passes over her head.

Overleaf: St Michael's Mount in 1895 (36179) St Michael's Mount, rising 230 feet above the sea, and crowned by the home of St Aubyn provides a spectacular backdrop to these gatherers of kelp, which farmers spread on the land as a valuable natural fertilizer.

Above: Newlyn Fish Market in 1920 (69747) On the edge of Newlyn's horseshoe-shaped fishing harbour was this fish market with the day's catch spread in neat heaps on the floor. Obviously, from the earnest discusssions taking place, the time had come for some hard bargaining.

Left: Newlyn in 1906 (56532) These Newlyn fishermen in their working clothes probably used their donkey cart to carry their catch to the fish market.

Opposite above: Water babies, Newlyn in 1893 (31800) Swimming costumes would have been considered an unnecessary sophistication by these little boys taking a dip in the harbour.

Opposite below: Newlyn Old Harbour in 1920 (69751) Between fishing and mending the nets there was little time for relaxation.

Above: The Longships Lighthouse, Lands End in 1928 (81218A) Nearly 300 miles from London and about 870 miles from John O'Groats, Lands End presents an awe inspiring granite bastion against the great might of Atlantic rollers. The lighthouse on the Longships Rock rises 123 feet from its rocky base to guide ships around this craggy and dangerous headland. Further offshore a ship with a large plume of smoke makes it way South towards the English Channel or France.

Left: First and Last House, Lands End in 1893 (31812) William Thomas proudly promotes this miniscule refuge as the first and last refreshment house in England. Outside the door, the empty shells of sea urchins and other marine creatures are being offered for sale. By 1928, as one can see from the photgraph above, the building had been substantially extended to accommodate the growing number of people who were able to make their way to this remote spot.

S T IVES. Courts and alleys lined with coloured stone cottages and a harbour crowded with fishing boats have inspired countless artists to paint in this pilchard fishing port. Among the Victorian artists who enjoyed painting here were Whistler and Sickert.

Right: Lifeboatmen at St Ives in 1906 (56543) Three tough lifeboatmen in bulky cork life jackets with their numbers emblazoned on their chests pose on the quay. Like Jerome K Jerome's *Three Men in a Boat* they are inseparable from their sharp eyed terrier.

Below: Gulls at St Ives in 1925 (78665) Gulls scavenge through the waste and help to keep the quay and beaches clean while visitors enjoy their time off watching others at work.

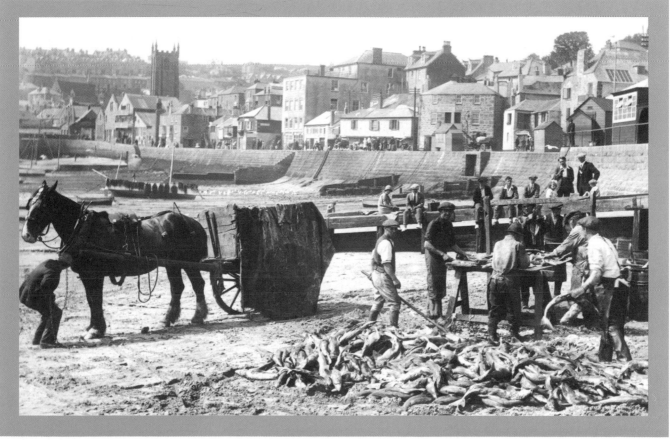

Top: The Fish Market at St Ives in 1925 (78659) After the catch had been auctioned, buyers carried it away in baskets. **Above: The Harbour at St Ives in 1925** (78658) The day's work was far from over when the boats brought the fish ashore. The catch still had to be gutted and packed in barrels. **Opposite: On the beach at St Ives in 1890** (24178) The little girls in this well behaved group were probably on a Sunday School outing. For many of them, it would be the only time that they travelled any distance from home.

CAMBORNE. With more than one hundred mines scattered in the surrounding countryside the twin towns of Camborne and Redruth were once at the heart of Cornwall's tin mining industry. The expansion of the industry was made possible by a native of Camborne, Richard Trevithick, who invented a steam engine which could pump water out of the pits from depths much greater than before.

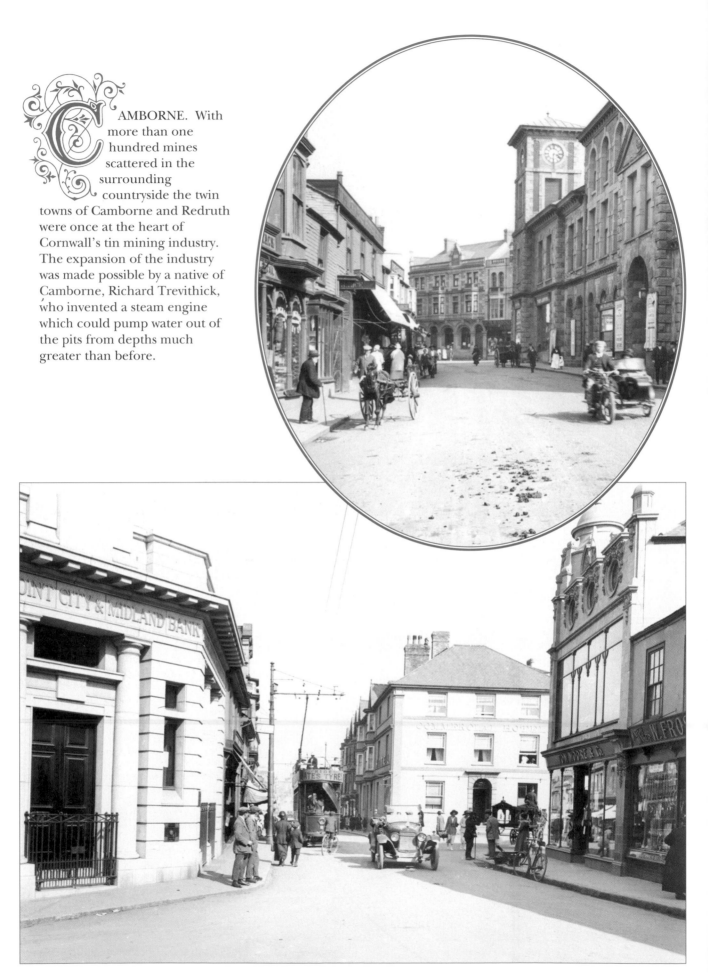

Top: Church Street, Camborne in 1922 (73299)   Pony carts and motor cycles mingled happily on Camborne's streets in the early 1920s. The imposing building on the right housed the Corn Exchange and, later, Knees Arcade. **Above: Trelowarren Street, Camborne in 1922** (73297)   An open-topped electric trolley bus advertising 'Bates Tyres' makes its way along Trelowarren Street from the London Joint City and Midland Bank towards The Commercial Hotel. Outside the hotel is an ornate horse-drawn hearse.

Above: Fore Street, Redruth in 1898
(41621) A sunny afternoon in this busy Cornish town. John Wesley preached from the balcony of Bank House, on the right and George Fox was imprisoned at the old inn. But it is William Murdoch, who lived here from 1782 to 1798, of whom Redruth is most proud. He invented gas lighting in this town, built a retort in his back garden and laid pipes into a living room. In 1792, his home became the first in the world to be lit by coal gas.

Left: Carn Brea, Redruth in 1906
(56456) On Carn Brea, the hill which separates Camborne from Redruth, stands this 14th century castle and a monument to Francis Basset, friend of the Cornish miner.

NEWQUAY is a town built on cliffs. For centuries it depended for its livelihood on pilchards and a man was deputed to watch from the headland for approaching shoals. When the town was a thriving port, pilots in long rowing boats known as gigs competed to be first to board incoming cargo ships and steer them through the shipping roads.

Right: Narrowcliffe, Newquay in 1938 (81262) Newquay's relaxed atmosphere and lovely clifftop walks made a holiday here the highlight of many people's lives.

Above: Tolcarne Beach, Newquay in 1930 (83057) Rocks, caves and golden sand turned Newquay from a tiny fishing hamlet into a very popular bathing resort. In the days before foreign holidays were commonplace, having a hut or tent on the beach was the height of luxury. Huts, particularly, were much sought after and had long waiting lists. **Previous page: Newquay Harbour in 1894** (33521) At low tide, large vessels heel over and dig into the mud alongside the quay used for unloading fish.

Above: Market Place, Padstow in 1906
(56268) This little town with narrow streets winding down to the shore seems to have been a favourite landing place for the early saints. St Patrick is said to have landed here in the 5th century and St Petrock, who was a Welshman, is said to have crossed from Ireland in a coracle to become the first to preach in the area. The photographer obviously chose a quiet day to visit Market Place where two men discuss the day's events near the newsagent's. Perhaps they were talking about the deputation representing half a million women which, in 1906, met the Prime Minister, Sir Henry Campbell-Bannerman, to press for women's right to the vote.

Left: Padstow Harbour in 1935 (87120) Alongside this busy little harbour are shops, hotels and warehouses. Outside Bray & Parker, 'builders, agricultural and general merchants' stand horses and waggons. The large poster on the left would not be allowed today as it is now illegal to advertise formula baby milk directly to mothers.

ADEBRIDGE. Until the 15th century, when Thomas Lovibond built the thirteen arch bridge which gave the town its name, crossing the River Camel could be an extremely hazardous business. It was, therefore, of such strategic importance during the Civil War that Cromwell felt impelled to come with 1500 men to take it. Often described as the 'longest and fairest bridge in Cornwall', it has a total span of about 320 feet.

Right: Wadebridge in 1935 (86678) A stylish Morgan three wheeler stops opposite the Molesworth Arms Hotel in Molesworth Street, which is proudly displaying its affiliation to both the AA and RAC. Motor cycle patrolmen of both these organisations were expected to give members a smart salute as they passed them on the road.

Above: Molesworth Street, Wadebridge in 1906 (56257) Outside the corner shop with its decorative lantern and advertisements for Cadbury's chocolate and cocoa, children counted their farthings to see if they had enough money to buy licquorice laces or sherbet dips. In the foreground, a little girl, her dress protected by a white pinafore, shows off her new sand bucket.

Above: Fore Street, Port Isaac in 1906
(56182) A jumble of fishermen's cottages
fall steeply down the main street until
their foundations are virtually in the sea.
Under many of these houses are fish
cellars where long ago fish were
preserved in salt before being transported
away for sale. Under a Great Western
Railway poster, advertising its excursion
pamphlet 'free at the company's railway
stations', is a sailor with a beard looking
very like the one in the Players cigarette
advertisement. A boy in short trousers
unself-consciously clutches a large posy of
flowers for his mother.

Left: Mending the nets in 1906 (56412)
For hardworking fishermen, clothing had
to be practical, with heavy oiled-wool
jerseys and long-lasting hob-nail boots.
But the style of hat was optional.

Overleaf: Port Isaac in 1895 (37024)
At low tide, the beach became a place of
work where boats and nets were repaired.

BOSCASTLE. Everyone who has walked the coastal path from Tintagel into Devon is familiar with Boscastle's little harbour lying in a narrow winding cleft between high cliffs. Built for the export of slate from the huge Delabole quarries nearby, the harbour is a wonderfully snug place to be in a storm. Nearby is the 'Devil's Bellows' - a blow-hole in the cliffs which throws out a cloud of spray.

Right: Wellington Hotel, Boscastle in 1906 (56171) Outside the hotel, a coach and horses is ready to set off, no doubt watched by the hotel's ostler who would have cared for the horses while they were rested.

Below: Boscastle Harbour and artists cottage in 1936 (87599) The slatey paths leading to the quay of this well-protected winding harbour made a wonderful rural promenade.

BUDE. In the 19th century, the town was notorious for wreckers who plundered ships that came to grief on its treacherous coast. More than eighty ships foundered in the area between 1824 and 1874 and in the church there is a figurehead of a ship, all that is left of a wreck in 1862 when most of the crew drowned. It is said that the roar of the surf on the long, sandy beaches which have made this resort a surfer's paradise can sometimes be heard ten miles inland.

Right: Falcon Hotel, Bude in 1920 (69508) In the early 19th century this canal was built to carry fertilizer inland and is now used for pleasure-boating and fishing. It was made redundant by the coming of the railway.

Above: Belle Vue, Bude in 1929 (82882) With the influx of visitors, ordinary houses were turned into shops and gardens were planted with palm trees. Isaac the chemist's enormous flag promoting his business would probably run into problems with the planning authorities today. The Rolls Royce standing in the car park opposite the Belle Vue Hotel suggests Bude had an affluent clientele.

ndex